The Zero Point Weight Loss Cookbook

Effortlessly Reach Your Weight Loss Goals Without Calorie Counting, Restrictions, or Stress!
Enjoy Indulgent, Guilt-Free Recipes and a 4-week Meal Plan

Kara Estrada

Copyright Notice

Disclaimer

The information contained in this book is intended for general informational purposes only and is not a substitute for professional advice. The author and publisher assume no responsibility for errors or omissions, or for damages resulting from the use or misuse of the information contained herein.

TABLE OF CONTENT

Introduction

Welcome to Zero Point Cooking

Step into a world where healthy eating doesn't mean deprivation, where deliciousness dances hand-in-hand with mindful choices, and where the journey to a healthier you is paved with vibrant flavors and culinary creativity. Welcome to the world of Zero Point Cooking!

This isn't just another diet cookbook. This is your passport to a sustainable lifestyle transformation, one where you'll discover the joy of nourishing your body with wholesome foods without ever feeling restricted. Forget the days of meticulously counting calories or banning entire food groups. Instead, embrace a liberating approach that celebrates abundance, empowers you with knowledge, and sets you free from the shackles of rigid diet plans.

Zero Point Cooking, inspired by the renowned WW (formerly Weight Watchers) program, is built upon a foundation of foods that are naturally low in calories and packed with essential nutrients. These "ZeroPoint heroes" – think vibrant fruits and vegetables, lean proteins, whole grains, and legumes – form the cornerstone of this culinary adventure. They are your culinary allies, offering unlimited possibilities for creating meals that are as satisfying as they are good for you.

Imagine starting your day with a burst of sunshine in a bowl, with a vibrant smoothie brimming with berries and spinach. Picture savoring a hearty lunch of grilled salmon over a bed of quinoa and roasted vegetables, the flavors mingling in a symphony of taste and texture. Envision ending your day with a comforting bowl of lentil soup, its warmth spreading through you like a culinary hug.

This is the promise of Zero Point Cooking. It's about rediscovering the pleasure of eating, not just for sustenance, but for joy, for exploration, and for the sheer delight of experiencing flavors that tantalize your taste buds while nourishing your body from the inside out.
But Zero Point Cooking is more than just a collection of recipes. It's a philosophy, a way of life that encourages you to:

- Prioritize whole, unprocessed foods: Embrace nature's bounty and savor the goodness of fresh ingredients.
- Listen to your body's cues: Learn to recognize true hunger and fullness, fostering a healthy relationship with food.
- Find joy in the cooking process: Transform your kitchen into a culinary playground, experimenting with flavors and textures.
- Cultivate a mindful approach to eating: Slow down, savor each bite, and appreciate the nourishment your food provides.

Within these pages, you'll find a treasure trove of culinary inspiration, from quick and easy weeknight meals to show-stopping dishes that will impress your guests. We'll guide you through the fundamentals of the Zero Point system, equip you with essential cooking techniques, and empower you to make informed choices that align with your individual needs and preferences.

This is your invitation to embark on a culinary adventure that will transform your relationship with food, your body, and yourself. So, open your mind, embrace the possibilities, and let the journey begin!

Understanding the Zero Point System

The Zero Point system, popularized by programs like WW (formerly Weight Watchers), is more than just a diet; it's a holistic approach to healthy eating that prioritizes nutrient-dense foods and mindful portion control.

By assigning a point value of zero to a wide range of nutritious options, it encourages a sustainable shift in dietary habits without the rigidity and deprivation often associated with traditional diets.

The Foundation: ZeroPoint Foods

At the core of the Zero Point system lies a carefully curated list of foods considered nutritional powerhouses. These ZeroPoint foods form the foundation of your eating plan and can be enjoyed freely without tracking or counting. They typically fall into the following categories:

- Fruits: A vibrant array of nature's candy, providing essential vitamins, minerals, and antioxidants. From berries bursting with flavor to tropical fruits brimming with sweetness, the options are endless.
- Vegetables: A diverse group offering a spectrum of nutrients and fiber, crucial for digestive health and satiety. Leafy greens, cruciferous vegetables, colorful peppers, and root vegetables are all included.
- Lean Proteins: Essential for building and repairing tissues, lean proteins also contribute to feelings of fullness. Skinless chicken and turkey breast, fish, eggs, tofu, and beans are excellent sources.
- Whole Grains: Packed with fiber and complex carbohydrates, whole grains provide sustained energy and help regulate blood sugar levels. Options include brown rice, quinoa, oats, and whole-wheat bread and pasta.

By emphasizing these nutrient-rich foods, the Zero Point system encourages a balanced diet that supports overall health and well-being.

The Framework: Points Budget and Mindful Eating

While ZeroPoint foods provide a foundation, the system acknowledges that a balanced diet also includes other foods. These foods are assigned points based on their nutritional value, considering factors like calories, saturated fat, sugar, and protein. You're given a daily or weekly points budget to spend, empowering you to make informed choices and practice portion control.

This framework encourages mindful eating, a practice that involves paying attention to your hunger cues, savoring each bite, and appreciating the flavors and textures of your food. By being present during meals, you can develop a healthier relationship with food and avoid overeating.

The Flexibility: Personalization and Adaptability

One of the strengths of the Zero Point system is its flexibility. Recognizing that individual needs and preferences vary, the program allows for personalization. You can adjust your points budget based on your goals, activity level, and dietary requirements.

Furthermore, the system adapts to various lifestyles and cultural preferences. Whether you're a vegetarian, follow a gluten-free diet, or have specific food allergies, you can find ZeroPoint options and recipes that fit your needs.

The Support: Community and Guidance

The Zero Point system often comes with a supportive community and resources to guide you on your journey. Workshops, online platforms, and personal coaching provide valuable tools and encouragement. These resources can help you stay motivated, overcome challenges, and develop long-term healthy habits.

The Science Behind the System

The Zero Point system is rooted in scientific principles of nutrition and behavior change. By prioritizing nutrient-dense foods, it promotes satiety and helps regulate blood sugar levels, reducing cravings and overeating. The points system encourages portion control and mindful eating, leading to a sustainable calorie deficit for weight loss.

Furthermore, the program's emphasis on support and community fosters a sense of accountability and encourages long-term adherence to healthy habits. Studies have shown that individuals who participate in structured weight-loss programs with support systems are more likely to achieve and maintain their weight-loss goals.

Beyond Weight Loss: A Holistic Approach to Health

While weight loss is often a primary goal, the Zero Point system offers benefits beyond shedding pounds. By focusing on nutrient-rich foods and mindful eating, it can improve overall health, including:

- Increased energy levels: A balanced diet provides the fuel your body needs to function optimally.
- Improved digestion: Fiber-rich ZeroPoint foods promote gut health and regular bowel movements.

- Reduced risk of chronic diseases: A healthy diet can lower your risk of developing conditions like heart disease, type 2 diabetes, and certain cancers.
- Enhanced mood and mental well-being: Studies have linked healthy eating patterns to improved mood and reduced symptoms of depression and anxiety.

Benefits of Zero Point Weight Loss

Zero point weight loss programs, like WW (formerly Weight Watchers), have revolutionized the way we approach healthy eating and weight management. By assigning a point value of zero to a wide array of nutritious foods, these programs offer a liberating and sustainable path towards achieving your wellness goals. Let's delve into the multifaceted benefits that this innovative approach provides:

1. Fostering a Foundation of Healthy Eating Habits:
At its core, the zero point system encourages a profound shift towards a diet rich in whole, unprocessed foods. By granting "free reign" to nutrient-dense powerhouses like fruits, vegetables, lean proteins, and whole grains, it nudges you towards a naturally healthier eating pattern. This focus on nutrient-rich choices helps to:
- Increase Fiber Intake: Promoting digestive health, blood sugar control, and feelings of fullness.
- Boost Vitamin and Mineral Consumption: Supporting overall health, immunity, and energy levels.
- Reduce Intake of Processed Foods: Minimizing consumption of unhealthy fats, added sugars, and sodium.

This foundation paves the way for long-term well-being, extending far beyond simple weight loss.

2. Simplifying the Weight Loss Journey:
Traditional calorie counting can be tedious and often unsustainable. The zero point system simplifies the process by eliminating the need to meticulously track every morsel of food. This liberation from constant calculations offers several key advantages:
- Reduced Stress and Obsession: Frees you from the mental burden of constant tracking, allowing you to focus on enjoying your food and the overall experience of eating.
- Increased Adherence: The simplicity of the system makes it easier to stick to, promoting long-term consistency and success.
- Greater Flexibility: Allows for spontaneity and enjoyment in your meals without derailing your progress.

This ease of use makes healthy eating a more integrated and enjoyable part of your lifestyle.

3. Promoting Mindful Eating and Portion Control:

While zero point foods can be enjoyed freely, the system still encourages mindful eating habits. By assigning points to other foods, it promotes a conscious awareness of portion sizes and overall calorie intake. This mindful approach fosters:

- Improved Self-Awareness: Encourages you to tune into your body's hunger and fullness cues.
- Enhanced Decision-Making: Empowers you to make informed choices about your food, considering both nutritional value and portion size.
- Sustainable Habits: Cultivates a balanced relationship with food, moving away from restrictive dieting towards mindful enjoyment.

This emphasis on mindful eating sets the stage for long-term healthy habits and a more positive relationship with food.

4. Cultivating a Supportive Environment for Success:

Many zero point weight loss programs offer a robust support system to guide and motivate you on your journey. This can include:

- Online Communities: Connecting with like-minded individuals for shared experiences, encouragement, and recipe ideas.
- Workshops and Group Meetings: Providing expert guidance, peer support, and accountability.
- Personal Coaching: Offering personalized advice, motivation, and strategies for overcoming challenges.

This supportive environment can be instrumental in fostering lasting success and navigating the inevitable hurdles along the way.

5. Achieving Sustainable Weight Loss and Improved Health:

Studies have consistently shown that zero point programs can lead to significant and sustainable weight loss. By promoting healthy eating habits, mindful portion control, and a supportive environment, these programs empower individuals to:

- Reach their Weight Goals: Achieving healthy and realistic weight loss outcomes.
- Improve Overall Health: Reducing risk factors for chronic diseases such as heart disease, type 2 diabetes, and certain cancers.
- Enhance Quality of Life: Boosting energy levels, mood, and self-confidence.

Tips for Success on Your Zero Point Journey

Congratulations on taking the first step towards a healthier, happier you with the ZeroPoint program! This journey is about more than just weight loss; it's about cultivating a sustainable lifestyle that nourishes your body and mind. To help you navigate this exciting path and achieve lasting success, we've compiled these comprehensive tips:

1. Embrace the Philosophy:
- Shift your mindset: ZeroPoint isn't a diet; it's a lifestyle shift. Focus on nourishing your body with wholesome foods and celebrating the abundance of ZeroPoint options.
- Prioritize progress over perfection: Don't get discouraged by occasional slip-ups. Every healthy choice you make is a victory. Focus on consistency and making progress over the long term.
- Cultivate mindful eating: Pay attention to your body's hunger and fullness cues. Savor each bite, eat slowly, and appreciate the flavors and textures of your food.

2. Master the Fundamentals:
- Know your ZeroPoint foods: Familiarize yourself with the extensive list of ZeroPoint foods, including fruits, vegetables, lean proteins, and whole grains. These are your nutritional powerhouses and the foundation of your eating plan.
- Understand the points system: While ZeroPoint foods are unlimited, other foods have associated points values. Learn how to track your points and make informed choices to stay within your budget.
- Hydrate consistently: Water is essential for overall health and can aid in weight management. Carry a water bottle with you throughout the day and aim for at least 8 glasses.

3. Build a Supportive Environment:
- Connect with your community: Join online forums, attend workshops, or find a ZeroPoint buddy for support, encouragement, and shared experiences.
- Involve your loved ones: Explain the program to your family and friends and enlist their support. Cooking together and sharing healthy meals can be a fun and bonding experience.
- Create a positive space: Surround yourself with things that inspire and motivate you. This could include motivational quotes, healthy cookbooks, or a vision board with your goals.

4. Plan for Success:

- Meal prep like a pro: Dedicate time each week to plan your meals and prep ingredients in advance. This will save you time and help you make healthier choices throughout the week.
- Stock your pantry and fridge: Keep your kitchen stocked with ZeroPoint staples and healthy snacks to avoid impulsive decisions when hunger strikes.
- Master the art of grocery shopping: Make a list before you go to the store and stick to it. Avoid processed foods and focus on fresh, whole ingredients.

5. Navigate Challenges with Grace:
- Dining out strategically: Research restaurant menus in advance or call ahead to inquire about ZeroPoint options. Don't be afraid to ask for modifications to make your meal healthier.
- Handle social situations mindfully: Plan ahead for parties and gatherings. Offer to bring a healthy dish to share and focus on socializing and enjoying the company of others.
- Overcome plateaus and setbacks: Weight loss isn't always linear. Don't get discouraged by plateaus. Reassess your habits, seek support, and stay focused on your long-term goals.

6. Celebrate Your Achievements:
- Acknowledge your progress: Track your successes, both big and small. Celebrate milestones, like reaching a weight loss goal or consistently making healthy choices.
- Reward yourself (wisely): Treat yourself to non-food rewards, like a massage, a new book, or a relaxing activity, to acknowledge your hard work and dedication.
- Embrace the journey: Remember that this is a lifelong commitment to your health and well-being. Enjoy the process, focus on building sustainable habits, and celebrate the positive changes you're making.

Pantry Essentials for Zero Point Cooking

Embarking on a ZeroPoint journey is akin to setting sail on a culinary adventure. Your pantry becomes your treasure chest, filled with provisions that nourish and delight without derailing your weight wellness goals. A well-stocked larder is the cornerstone of effortless and inspired ZeroPoint cooking, ensuring you have the building blocks for flavor and satisfaction readily at hand.

The Foundation: ZeroPoint Heroes

These are the stalwarts of your ZeroPoint pantry, the ingredients you can turn to again and again for meals that are both delicious and guilt-free:

- Fruits: A vibrant array of nature's candy. Stock up on fresh seasonal favorites and frozen varieties for smoothies, snacks, and desserts. Apples, bananas, berries, and citrus fruits are versatile choices.
- Vegetables: The backbone of any healthy diet. Fresh, frozen, and canned (no-salt-added) vegetables provide endless possibilities. Leafy greens, cruciferous vegetables, and colorful peppers are must-haves.
- Lean Proteins: Essential for satiety and muscle maintenance. Chicken breasts, fish fillets, turkey, and eggs are excellent sources. Canned tuna and salmon (packed in water) are convenient options.
- Whole Grains: Complex carbohydrates that provide sustained energy. Oats, quinoa, brown rice, and whole-wheat bread and pasta offer fiber and nutrients.

Flavor Boosters: Spices & Herbs

A symphony of flavors awaits with a well-curated spice rack. These aromatic additions elevate your dishes without adding points:

- Essential Spices: Salt, black pepper, garlic powder, onion powder, paprika, and red pepper flakes are indispensable for seasoning.
- Aromatic Herbs: Dried basil, oregano, thyme, rosemary, and parsley add depth and complexity to your cooking.
- Global Flavors: Explore the world of spices with cumin, turmeric, coriander, ginger, and cinnamon for exciting culinary adventures.

Pantry Staples: The Supporting Cast

These essential ingredients provide the foundation for countless ZeroPoint creations:

- Healthy Fats: Extra virgin olive oil, avocado oil, and nuts and seeds (in moderation) provide essential fatty acids and enhance flavor.
- Vinegars: Balsamic, red wine, apple cider, and white wine vinegars add zest and brightness to dressings and marinades.
- Broths & Stocks: Low-sodium or homemade broths and stocks form the base for soups, stews, and sauces.
- Condiments: Mustard, hot sauce, soy sauce (low-sodium), and salsa add flavor without excessive points.
- Sweeteners: Artificial sweeteners and sugar substitutes can be used in moderation to satisfy your sweet tooth.

Beyond the Basics: Enhancing Your Culinary Arsenal

Elevate your ZeroPoint cooking with these additions:

- Beans & Legumes: Canned beans (no-salt-added) like black beans, chickpeas, and kidney beans are packed with protein and fiber.
- Non-Dairy Milk: Unsweetened almond milk, soy milk, or coconut milk offer versatility for beverages and cooking.
- Flavor Enhancers: Lemon and lime juice, fresh ginger, garlic, and onions add zest and depth to dishes.
- Thickeners: Cornstarch, arrowroot powder, and xanthan gum help create sauces and gravies without added points.

Organization is Key:

A well-organized pantry is a joy to navigate. Utilize clear containers, labels, and shelf risers to maximize space and keep ingredients visible. Regularly check expiration dates and practice FIFO (First In, First Out) to minimize waste.

A Note on Portion Control:

Even with ZeroPoint foods, mindful eating is crucial. Be aware of serving sizes and listen to your body's hunger cues.

CHAPTER 1

Breakfast Bliss

1.1 Zero Point Power Bowls

Berry Blast Smoothie Bowl

Start your day with a burst of flavor and a boost of nutrients with this vibrant and satisfying Berry Blast Smoothie Bowl. Packed with ZeroPoint fruits, this recipe is a delicious and guilt-free way to fuel your morning.

YIELDS: 1 SERVING PREP TIME: 5 MINUTES BLEND TIME: 1 MINUTE

Ingredients:
- 1 cup frozen mixed berries (strawberries, raspberries, blueberries, blackberries)
- 1/2 cup unsweetened almond milk (or any other ZeroPoint milk)
- 1/2 frozen banana, sliced
- 1/4 cup non-fat plain Greek yogurt (optional, adds a creamy texture)
- 1 tablespoon chia seeds (optional, for added fiber and omega-3s)

Toppings (optional, choose ZeroPoint options):
- Fresh berries
- Sliced banana
- A sprinkle of chopped nuts (in moderation)
- A drizzle of sugar-free syrup (in moderation)
- Unsweetened shredded coconut

Equipment:
- High-speed blender
- Serving bowl
- Spoon

Instructions:
1. Combine & Blend: In your blender, combine the frozen berries, almond milk, frozen banana slices, Greek yogurt (if using), and chia seeds (if using).
2. Achieve Desired Consistency: Blend on high speed until smooth and creamy. If the mixture is too thick, add a splash more almond milk. If it's too thin, add a few more frozen berries.
3. Pour & Decorate: Pour the smoothie mixture into your serving bowl.
4. Top & Enjoy: Get creative with your toppings! Arrange fresh berries, banana slices, a sprinkle of nuts, or a drizzle of sugar-free syrup. Enjoy immediately.

Tips & Variations:
- Fruit Variety: Feel free to experiment with different types of frozen berries. Mango chunks or pineapple can also add a tropical twist.
- Thickness: For a thicker smoothie bowl, use less almond milk or add a few ice cubes.
- Sweetness: If you prefer a sweeter smoothie bowl, add a ripe banana or a touch of your preferred ZeroPoint sweetener.
- Protein Boost: Add a scoop of protein powder to your smoothie for an extra boost of protein and a thicker texture.
- Make it Ahead: Prepare the smoothie mixture the night before and store it in the refrigerator. In the morning, give it a quick blend and top with your favorite ingredients.

Why this recipe is a ZeroPoint winner:
- Nutrient-Dense: Bursting with vitamins, minerals, and antioxidants from the berries.
- High in Fiber: Promotes digestive health and keeps you feeling full.
- Naturally Sweet: Satisfies your sweet cravings without added sugars.
- Versatile: Customize with your favorite toppings for endless variations.

Tropical Paradise Smoothie Bowl

Transport yourself to a tropical paradise with this vibrant and refreshing smoothie bowl. Packed with a medley of ZeroPoint fruits and a creamy texture, this recipe is a delicious and guilt-free way to start your day or enjoy a healthy snack.

YIELDS: 1 SERVING PREP TIME: 5 MINUTES BLEND TIME: 1 MINUTE

Ingredients:

- ½ cup frozen mixed berries (strawberries, raspberries, blueberries)
- ½ cup frozen mango chunks
- ½ cup frozen pineapple chunks
- ½ frozen banana, sliced
- ½ cup unsweetened coconut milk (or any other ZeroPoint milk)
- ¼ cup non-fat plain Greek yogurt
- 1 tablespoon chia seeds (optional, for added fiber and omega-3s)

Toppings (optional, choose ZeroPoint options):

- Fresh berries
- Sliced banana or mango
- A sprinkle of unsweetened shredded coconut
- A drizzle of sugar-free syrup (in moderation)
- Chopped macadamia nuts (in moderation)
- A few fresh mint leaves

Equipment:

- High-speed blender
- Serving bowl
- Spoon

Instructions:
1. **Combine:** In your blender, combine the frozen mixed berries, mango chunks, pineapple chunks, banana slices, coconut milk, Greek yogurt, and chia seeds (if using).
2. **Blend:** Blend on high speed until smooth and creamy. If the mixture is too thick, add a splash more coconut milk. If it's too thin, add a few more frozen berries or a few ice cubes.
3. **Pour:** Pour the smoothie mixture into your serving bowl.
4. **Top & Enjoy:** Decorate your Tropical Paradise Smoothie Bowl with fresh fruit, a sprinkle of coconut, a drizzle of sugar-free syrup, and a few fresh mint leaves. Enjoy immediately!

Tips & Variations:
- **Fruit Fusion:** Feel free to experiment with other ZeroPoint fruits like papaya or passion fruit.
- **Creamy Dreamy:** For an extra creamy texture, add a quarter of a ripe avocado to the blender.
- **Sweetness:** If you prefer a sweeter smoothie bowl, add a ripe banana or a touch of your preferred ZeroPoint sweetener.
- **Tropical Twist:** Add a squeeze of lime juice for a tangy kick.
- **Make it Ahead:** Prepare the smoothie mixture the night before and store it in the refrigerator. In the morning, give it a quick blend and top with your favorite ingredients.

Why this recipe is a ZeroPoint winner:
- **Nutrient-Dense:** Loaded with vitamins, minerals, and antioxidants from the variety of fruits.
- **High in Fiber:** Promotes digestive health and keeps you feeling full and satisfied.
- **Naturally Sweet:** Satisfies your sweet cravings without added sugars.
- **Versatile:** Customize with your favorite toppings for endless variations.
- **Hydrating:** The coconut milk and fruits contribute to your daily fluid intake.

Savory Oatmeal Power Bowl with Eggs

This savory oatmeal bowl is a powerhouse of ZeroPoint nutrition, offering a creamy texture, a burst of berry goodness, and a savory twist to your morning routine.

Ingredients:
- 1/2 cup rolled oats (not instant)
- 1 cup unsweetened almond milk (or any other ZeroPoint milk)
- 1/4 cup water
- 1/4 teaspoon salt
- 1/4 teaspoon black pepper
- 1/2 cup mixed berries (fresh or frozen)
- 1 large egg
- 1/2 teaspoon olive oil (optional, for added richness)

Toppings (optional, choose ZeroPoint options):
- More fresh berries
- Sliced banana or apple
- A sprinkle of chopped nuts (in moderation)
- A dollop of non-fat plain Greek yogurt
- Hot sauce (for extra zest)

Instructions:
1. Cook the Oats: In a small saucepan, combine oats, almond milk, water, salt, and pepper. Bring to a simmer over medium heat, then reduce heat and cook for 3-5 minutes, or until the oats are creamy and cooked through. Stir occasionally to prevent sticking.

2. Sauté the Berries: While the oats are cooking, heat the olive oil (if using) in a small skillet over medium heat. Add the mixed berries and sauté for 2-3 minutes, or until they soften and release their juices.
3. Cook the Egg: In a separate small skillet, cook the egg to your liking (fried, scrambled, or poached).
4. Assemble the Bowl: Pour the cooked oatmeal into a bowl. Top with the sautéed berries and cooked egg.
5. Add Toppings & Enjoy: Add your favorite ZeroPoint toppings and enjoy immediately.

Variations:
- Spice it Up: Add a pinch of red pepper flakes or a dash of hot sauce to the oatmeal for a spicy kick.
- Greens: Stir in a handful of spinach or kale during the last minute of cooking the oats for added nutrients.
- Protein Boost: For extra protein, add a scoop of protein powder to the cooked oatmeal or top with a few slices of lean ham or turkey.
- Sweet and Savory: For a touch of sweetness, add a drizzle of sugar-free maple syrup or a sprinkle of cinnamon to the oatmeal.

Tips for Success:
- Oat Choice: Use rolled oats or steel-cut oats for a heartier texture. Avoid instant oats, as they tend to be more processed.
- Creamy Texture: For extra creaminess, use a combination of almond milk and water or add a splash of non-fat plain Greek yogurt to the cooked oatmeal.
- Berry Variety: Use a mix of your favorite berries for a variety of flavors and textures.
- Seasoning: Don't be afraid to experiment with different seasonings. Garlic powder, onion powder, or dried herbs can add depth of flavor.

Why this recipe is a ZeroPoint winner:
- Nutrient-Dense: Packed with fiber, protein, vitamins, and antioxidants.
- Satisfying: The combination of complex carbohydrates, protein, and healthy fats keeps you feeling full and energized.
- Versatile: Easily customizable with your favorite toppings and variations.
- Quick & Easy: Perfect for busy mornings.

Southwest Quinoa Power Bowl

This vibrant and satisfying Southwest Quinoa Power Bowl is a ZeroPoint winner! Packed with protein, fiber, and healthy fats, it will keep you feeling full and energized for hours. The creamy avocado and the burst of sweetness from the mixed berries add a delightful touch.

YIELDS: 1 SERVING PREP TIME: 10-15 MINUTES COOK TIME: 20 MINUTES

Ingredients:
- For the Quinoa:
  - 1/2 cup uncooked quinoa
  - 1 cup water
  - 1/4 teaspoon salt (optional)
- For the Bowl:
  - 1/2 cup cooked black beans (no salt added)
  - 1/2 cup frozen corn
  - 1/4 cup chopped red onion
  - 1/4 cup chopped bell pepper (any color)
  - 1/4 cup chopped cilantro
  - 1/2 ripe avocado, diced
  - 1/2 cup mixed berries (strawberries, raspberries, blueberries, blackberries)
- For the Dressing:
  - 2 tablespoons lime juice
  - 1 tablespoon extra virgin olive oil
  - 1/2 teaspoon ground cumin
  - 1/4 teaspoon chili powder
  - Pinch of cayenne pepper (optional)

Instructions:
1. Cook the Quinoa: Rinse the quinoa in a fine-mesh sieve. Combine quinoa, water, and salt (if using) in a small saucepan. Bring to a boil, then reduce heat and simmer, covered, for 15-20 minutes, or until the water is absorbed and the quinoa is cooked through. Fluff with a fork.
2. Assemble the Bowl: In a serving bowl, layer the cooked quinoa, black beans, corn, red onion, bell pepper, and cilantro.
3. Prepare the Dressing: In a small bowl, whisk together lime juice, olive oil, cumin, chili powder, and cayenne pepper (if using).
4. Add the Creamy Texture: Gently fold in the diced avocado.
5. Top with Berries and Dressing: Top the bowl with mixed berries and drizzle with the dressing.

Optional Toppings/Variations:
- Protein Boost: Add grilled chicken or fish for extra protein.
- Spice it Up: Include chopped jalapeños or a dash of hot sauce for extra heat.
- Greens: Add a handful of spinach or kale for extra nutrients.
- Crunchy Texture: Top with a sprinkle of chopped walnuts or pumpkin seeds (in moderation).

Tips for Success:
- Rinsing Quinoa: Rinsing quinoa before cooking helps remove any bitter taste.
- Perfectly Cooked Quinoa: For fluffy quinoa, use a 2:1 ratio of water to quinoa.
- Dressing Consistency: Adjust the amount of olive oil to achieve your desired dressing consistency.
- Freshness: Use fresh ingredients whenever possible for the best flavor.

Why this recipe is a ZeroPoint winner:
- Packed with ZeroPoint Foods: Quinoa, black beans, corn, fruits, and vegetables are all ZeroPoint foods.
- Nutrient-Dense: Provides a good source of protein, fiber, vitamins, and minerals.
- Balanced Meal: Offers a healthy balance of carbohydrates, protein, and healthy fats.
- Flavorful and Satisfying: The combination of flavors and textures makes this bowl a delicious and satisfying meal.

1.2 Egg-cellent Creations

Spinach and Feta Omelet

This recipe elevates the classic spinach and feta omelet with a burst of berry goodness. Enjoy a symphony of flavors and textures while staying true to your ZeroPoint goals.

YIELDS: 1 SERVING PREP TIME: 5 MINUTES COOK TIME: 5-7 MINUTES

Ingredients:
- 1 teaspoon olive oil
- 1 cup fresh spinach, chopped
- 2 large eggs
- 1 tablespoon unsweetened almond milk (or any other ZeroPoint milk)
- 1/4 cup crumbled feta cheese
- Salt and black pepper to taste

- 1/2 cup mixed berries (strawberries, raspberries, blueberries, blackberries)

Optional toppings:
- Fresh herbs (dill, parsley, chives)
- A dollop of plain non-fat Greek yogurt
- Hot sauce (if desired)

Equipment:
- Non-stick skillet
- Spatula

Instructions:

1. Sauté the Spinach: Heat olive oil in a non-stick skillet over medium heat. Add the chopped spinach and sauté until wilted, about 2 minutes. Season with salt and black pepper.
2. Whisk the Eggs: In a bowl, whisk together the eggs and almond milk. Season with salt and black pepper.
3. Cook the Omelet: Pour the egg mixture into the skillet with the spinach. Let it cook undisturbed for a minute or two until the edges begin to set.
4. Add the Feta & Berries: Sprinkle the crumbled feta cheese over one half of the omelet. Top with the mixed berries.
5. Fold & Finish: Gently fold the omelet in half, covering the feta and berries. Cook for another minute or two until the cheese is melted and the eggs are cooked through.
6. Serve & Enjoy: Slide the omelet onto a plate. Garnish with fresh herbs and a dollop of Greek yogurt, if desired.

Tips for Success:
- Even Cooking: Use a low to medium heat to prevent the omelet from browning too quickly or burning.
- Creamy Texture: Adding a tablespoon of almond milk to the eggs creates a creamier texture.
- Non-Stick Skillet: A good quality non-stick skillet is essential for preventing the omelet from sticking.
- Fresh Berries: Use fresh, ripe berries for the best flavor and texture.
- Don't Overcrowd: Avoid overcrowding the pan with too much spinach, as this will make it difficult to cook the omelet evenly.

Variations:
- Spice it Up: Add a pinch of red pepper flakes to the egg mixture for a spicy kick.
- Veggie Boost: Include other ZeroPoint vegetables like mushrooms, onions, or peppers.
- Cheese Choices: Experiment with different types of ZeroPoint cheeses like cottage cheese or ricotta.

Why this recipe is a ZeroPoint winner:
- Protein-Packed: Eggs provide a great source of protein, keeping you feeling full and satisfied.
- Nutrient-Rich: Spinach and berries offer essential vitamins, minerals, and antioxidants.
- Low in Calories: This omelet is a light and healthy breakfast option that won't derail your ZeroPoint progress.
- Flavorful: The combination of spinach, feta, and mixed berries creates a delicious and satisfying flavor profile.

Smoked Salmon and Avocado Scramble

This recipe elevates the classic scrambled eggs to a gourmet, ZeroPoint breakfast experience. The creamy avocado complements the smoky salmon beautifully, while the vibrant mixed berries add a refreshing burst of sweetness and antioxidants.

YIELDS: 1 SERVING PREP TIME: 5 MINUTES COOK TIME: 5 MINUTES

Ingredients:
- For the Scramble:
  - 1 large egg
  - 1 egg white
  - 1 tablespoon unsweetened almond milk (or any other ZeroPoint milk)
  - Salt and black pepper to taste
  - 1/4 avocado, mashed
  - 1 ounce smoked salmon, chopped
  - 1 teaspoon chopped fresh dill (optional)

- For the Berry Burst:
  - 1/2 cup mixed berries (strawberries, raspberries, blueberries, blackberries)
  - 1 teaspoon lemon juice (optional, enhances the berry flavor)

Equipment:
- Non-stick skillet
- Spatula
- Small bowl

Instructions:

1. Prepare the Berries: In a small bowl, gently toss the mixed berries with lemon juice (if using). Set aside.
2. Whisk the Eggs: In a separate bowl, whisk together the egg, egg white, almond milk, salt, and pepper.
3. Cook the Eggs: Heat the non-stick skillet over medium heat. Pour in the egg mixture and cook, stirring frequently with a spatula, until the eggs are set but still slightly creamy.
4. Assemble: Remove the skillet from the heat. Gently fold in the mashed avocado, chopped smoked salmon, and fresh dill (if using).
5. Plate & Serve: Transfer the scramble to a plate and top with the prepared mixed berries. Enjoy immediately.

Optional Toppings/Variations:

- Spice it up: Add a pinch of red pepper flakes to the scramble for a hint of heat.
- Herby Twist: Incorporate chopped chives or parsley into the scramble for an extra layer of flavor.
- Creamy Indulgence: For an even richer texture, add a dollop of plain non-fat Greek yogurt to the scramble.
- Veggie Boost: Sauté some spinach or mushrooms and add them to the scramble for extra nutrients.

Tips for Success:

- Avocado Ripeness: Use a ripe but firm avocado for optimal creaminess.
- Salmon Quality: Choose good quality smoked salmon for the best flavor.
- Don't Overcook: Cook the eggs gently to prevent them from becoming dry.
- Fresh Berries: Use fresh, seasonal berries for the most vibrant flavor and texture.

Why this recipe is a ZeroPoint winner:

- Protein Packed: Provides a good source of protein from the eggs and smoked salmon to keep you full and satisfied.
- Healthy Fats: Avocado contributes healthy monounsaturated fats, which are beneficial for heart health.
- Nutrient-Rich: The mixed berries offer a wealth of vitamins, minerals, and antioxidants.
- Flavorful & Satisfying: A delicious combination of flavors and textures that will make you look forward to breakfast.

Veggie-Packed Frittata

This vibrant frittata is a symphony of flavors and textures, bursting with fresh vegetables and the sweetness of mixed berries. It's a hearty and satisfying ZeroPoint breakfast that will fuel your morning and delight your taste buds.

YIELDS: 4 SERVINGS PREP TIME: 15 MINUTES COOK TIME: 25-30 MINUTES

Ingredients:

- 1 tablespoon olive oil
- 1 small onion, chopped
- 2 cloves garlic, minced
- 1 cup chopped bell peppers (any color)
- 1 cup chopped broccoli florets
- 1 cup chopped spinach
- 1 cup sliced mushrooms
- 1/2 cup chopped fresh tomatoes
- 1/2 cup mixed berries (such as blueberries, raspberries, and blackberries)
- 8 large eggs
- 1/4 cup unsweetened almond milk (or any other ZeroPoint milk)
- 1/4 cup grated Parmesan cheese (optional)
- Salt and black pepper to taste

Equipment:

- Large oven-safe skillet (cast iron or non-stick)
- Mixing bowl
- Whisk

Instructions:

1. **Sauté the Veggies:** Preheat your oven to 350°F (175°C). Heat the olive oil in the skillet over medium heat. Add the onion and garlic and cook until softened, about 5 minutes. Add the bell peppers, broccoli, spinach, and mushrooms. Cook until the vegetables are tender-crisp, about 5 minutes more.
2. **Whisk the Eggs:** In a mixing bowl, whisk together the eggs, almond milk, Parmesan cheese (if using), salt, and pepper.
3. **Combine and Bake:** Pour the egg mixture over the vegetables in the skillet. Stir in the chopped tomatoes and mixed berries. Transfer the skillet to the preheated oven and bake for 25-30 minutes, or until the frittata is set and golden brown.
4. **Cool and Serve:** Let the frittata cool slightly before slicing and serving.

Optional Toppings/Variations:

- **Herbs:** Add fresh herbs like chopped basil, parsley, or chives to the egg mixture for extra flavor.
- **Spice:** Sprinkle in a pinch of red pepper flakes for a touch of heat.
- **Cheese:** For a creamier frittata, add a dollop of ricotta cheese or cottage cheese to the egg mixture.
- **Meat:** If you have points to spare, you can add cooked chicken sausage, bacon crumbles, or ham to the frittata.

Tips for Success:

- **Even Cooking:** For even cooking, make sure your vegetables are chopped into similar sizes.
- **Don't Overcrowd:** Avoid overcrowding the skillet with too many vegetables, as this can make the frittata watery.
- **Check for Doneness:** The frittata is done when the center is set and a knife inserted comes out clean.
- **Storage:** Leftovers can be stored in the refrigerator for up to 3 days.

Why this recipe is a ZeroPoint winner:

- **Packed with Nutrients:** Loaded with vitamins, minerals, and antioxidants from the vegetables and berries.
- **High in Protein:** Provides a good source of protein from the eggs, keeping you feeling full and satisfied.
- **Versatile:** Can be customized with different vegetables, herbs, and spices to suit your taste.
- **Great for Meal Prep:** Make a large frittata and enjoy it for breakfast throughout the week.

Mushroom and Gruyere Quiche

This quiche is a symphony of flavors and textures, boasting a creamy, savory filling studded with earthy mushrooms and nutty Gruyere cheese, all complemented by a burst of sweetness from mixed berries. It's a ZeroPoint-friendly dish that's perfect for a leisurely brunch or a satisfying light meal.

YIELDS: 6 SERVINGS PREP TIME: 20 MINUTES COOK TIME: 40-45 MINUTES

Ingredients:
- For the crust:
  - 1 cup whole wheat flour
  - 1/4 cup rolled oats
  - 1/4 teaspoon salt
  - 4 tablespoons cold unsalted butter, cubed
  - 4-6 tablespoons ice water
- For the filling:
  - 1 tablespoon olive oil
  - 1 cup sliced mushrooms (cremini, shiitake, or a mix)
  - 1 small onion, chopped
  - 2 cloves garlic, minced

- 4 large eggs
- 1 cup unsweetened almond milk
- 1/2 cup grated Gruyere cheese
- 1/4 cup chopped fresh mixed berries (strawberries, raspberries, blueberries)
- 1/4 teaspoon salt
- 1/4 teaspoon black pepper
- Pinch of nutmeg

Equipment:
- 9-inch pie dish
- Mixing bowls
- Whisk
- Non-stick skillet

Instructions:

1. Prepare the crust: In a bowl, combine flour, oats, and salt. Cut in butter until mixture resembles coarse crumbs. Gradually add ice water, mixing until dough forms a ball. Wrap and refrigerate for 30 minutes.
2. Preheat and pre-bake: Preheat oven to 375°F (190°C). Roll out dough and line the pie dish. Prick the bottom with a fork and bake for 10-12 minutes until lightly golden.
3. Sauté the vegetables: While the crust is baking, heat olive oil in a skillet. Sauté mushrooms and onions until softened, about 5 minutes. Add garlic and cook for 1 minute more.
4. Whisk the filling: In a bowl, whisk eggs, almond milk, Gruyere cheese, salt, pepper, and nutmeg. Stir in the sautéed vegetables and berries.
5. Assemble and bake: Pour the filling into the pre-baked crust. Bake for 30-35 minutes, or until the center is set and the top is lightly golden.
6. Cool and serve: Let the quiche cool for 10 minutes before slicing and serving.

Optional toppings/variations:

- Herbs: Add fresh herbs like thyme, rosemary, or chives to the filling.
- Spices: A pinch of smoked paprika or cayenne pepper can add a subtle kick.
- Cheese: Experiment with other ZeroPoint cheeses like feta or part-skim mozzarella.
- Vegetables: Add other ZeroPoint vegetables like spinach, bell peppers, or zucchini.

Tips for success:

- Blind bake the crust: This prevents a soggy bottom.
- Don't overfill: Leave some space at the top of the crust to prevent spilling.
- Check for doneness: Insert a toothpick into the center; it should come out clean when the quiche is done.
- Rest before slicing: This allows the filling to set and prevents it from crumbling.

Why this recipe is a ZeroPoint winner:

- Packed with protein: Eggs provide a good source of protein for satiety.
- Rich in nutrients: Mushrooms offer vitamins and minerals, while berries provide antioxidants.
- Satisfying and flavorful: The combination of savory and sweet flavors creates a balanced and delicious meal.
- Versatile: Enjoy it for breakfast, brunch, lunch, or even a light dinner.

1.3 Quick & Easy Breakfasts

Overnight Oats with Berries and Nuts

Wake up to a breakfast that's both delicious and nutritious with this ZeroPoint Overnight Oats recipe. Packed with a variety of mixed berries and a lusciously creamy texture, it's the perfect way to start your day.

YIELDS: 1 SERVING PREP TIME: 5 MINUTES COOK TIME: NONE (OVERNIGHT REFRIGERATION)

Ingredients:
- 1/2 cup rolled oats (not instant)
- 1 cup unsweetened almond milk (or any other ZeroPoint milk)
- 1/4 cup non-fat plain Greek yogurt
- 1/4 cup mixed berries (fresh or frozen)
- 1 tablespoon chia seeds
- 1/2 teaspoon vanilla extract
- 2 tablespoons chopped walnuts (or other ZeroPoint nuts)

Optional toppings:
- Additional fresh berries
- A drizzle of sugar-free maple syrup (in moderation)
- A sprinkle of cinnamon
- A dollop of almond butter (in moderation)

Instructions:
1. Combine ingredients: In a jar or container with a lid, combine the oats, almond milk, Greek yogurt, mixed berries, chia seeds, and vanilla extract.
2. Stir and seal: Stir well to ensure all ingredients are evenly distributed. Seal the container tightly.
3. Refrigerate overnight: Place the container in the refrigerator for at least 2 hours, or preferably overnight.
4. Top and enjoy: In the morning, top with your favorite additions like additional fresh berries, a drizzle of sugar-free maple syrup, a sprinkle of cinnamon, or a dollop of almond butter. Enjoy cold.

Tips for success:
- Oats: Use rolled oats or old-fashioned oats for the best texture. Instant oats can become mushy.
- Milk: Any ZeroPoint milk works well. Adjust the amount for desired consistency.
- Berries: Use a mix of your favorite berries for a variety of flavors and antioxidants.
- Chia seeds: Chia seeds add a pudding-like texture and boost the fiber content.
- Sweetness: If you prefer a sweeter oatmeal, add a ripe banana or a touch of your preferred ZeroPoint sweetener.
- Make-ahead: This recipe can be made in advance for a grab-and-go breakfast throughout the week.

Why this recipe is a ZeroPoint winner:
- Nutrient-rich: Provides a healthy dose of fiber, protein, vitamins, and antioxidants.
- Filling and satisfying: Keeps you feeling full and energized throughout the morning.
- Naturally sweet: Satisfies your sweet cravings without added sugars.
- Versatile: Customize with your favorite toppings for endless variations.
- Convenient: Perfect for busy mornings or meal prepping.

Yogurt Parfaits with Granola and Fruit

This parfait is a delightful and effortless way to enjoy a ZeroPoint breakfast or snack. The combination of creamy yogurt, fresh berries, and crunchy granola creates a symphony of textures and flavors that will keep you satisfied and energized.

YIELDS: 1 SERVING PREP TIME: 5 MINUTES COOK TIME: NONE

Ingredients:

- 1 cup non-fat plain Greek yogurt (for extra creaminess)
- ½ cup mixed berries (strawberries, raspberries, blueberries, blackberries)
- ¼ cup whole grain granola (choose a variety with no added sugars)
- 1 tablespoon chia seeds (optional, for added fiber and omega-3s)

Optional Toppings (ZeroPoint):

- A drizzle of sugar-free maple syrup or honey (in moderation)
- A sprinkle of cinnamon
- A few chopped nuts (in moderation)
- Unsweetened shredded coconut

Instructions:

1. Layer the Base: In a glass or bowl, start with a layer of Greek yogurt.
2. Add Berries: Top the yogurt with a layer of mixed berries.
3. Sprinkle Granola: Sprinkle a layer of granola over the berries.
4. Repeat Layers: Repeat the layers of yogurt, berries, and granola until you reach the top of your container.
5. Top it Off: Finish with your favorite ZeroPoint toppings, such as a drizzle of sugar-free syrup, a sprinkle of cinnamon, or a few chopped nuts.
6. Enjoy Immediately: Grab a spoon and savor the delightful combination of flavors and textures.

Tips for Extra Creaminess:

- Greek Yogurt: Opt for plain, non-fat Greek yogurt for its naturally thick and creamy texture.
- Chill Ingredients: Using chilled yogurt and berries enhances the creamy consistency of the parfait.
- Layering Technique: Create distinct layers for a visually appealing and texturally satisfying parfait.
- Chia Seeds: Adding chia seeds creates a pudding-like texture as they absorb moisture from the yogurt.

Variations:

- Fruit Fusion: Explore different fruit combinations like sliced bananas, peaches, or mangoes.
- Spice it Up: Add a pinch of cinnamon or nutmeg for a warm, comforting flavor.
- Protein Boost: Incorporate a scoop of protein powder into the yogurt for an extra protein punch.
- Make it Tropical: Use coconut yogurt and top with tropical fruits like mango and pineapple.

Why this recipe is a ZeroPoint Winner:

- Nutrient-Rich: Packed with protein, calcium, antioxidants, and fiber.
- Naturally Sweet: Satisfies your sweet cravings with the natural sugars found in fruits.
- Versatile: Easily customizable with various fruits, toppings, and flavors.
- Quick & Easy: Requires minimal prep time, making it perfect for busy mornings.

Whole Wheat Toast with Avocado and Tomato

This recipe transforms ordinary whole wheat toast into a delightful and nutritious ZeroPoint breakfast or snack. The creamy avocado paired with the sweetness of mixed berries creates a symphony of flavors and textures that will tantalize your taste buds.

YIELDS: 1 SERVING PREP TIME: 5 MINUTES COOK TIME: 5 MINUTES

Ingredients:
- 1 slice whole wheat bread
- 1/4 ripe avocado, mashed
- 1/4 cup mixed berries (strawberries, blueberries, raspberries, blackberries), finely chopped
- 1/2 teaspoon lime juice
- Pinch of salt
- Pinch of black pepper

Optional toppings:
- Everything bagel seasoning
- Red pepper flakes
- Fresh cilantro, chopped

Equipment:
- Toaster or skillet
- Small bowl
- Fork

Instructions:

1. Toast the bread: Toast the whole wheat bread to your desired level of crispness.
2. Prepare the berry salsa: In a small bowl, combine the chopped mixed berries with lime juice, salt, and pepper. Mix gently.
3. Assemble: Spread the mashed avocado evenly over the toasted bread. Top with the prepared berry salsa.
4. Garnish (optional): Sprinkle with everything bagel seasoning, red pepper flakes, or chopped cilantro for an extra layer of flavor.

Tips for success:

- Bread choice: Choose a whole wheat bread with at least 3 grams of fiber per slice.
- Avocado ripeness: Use a ripe but firm avocado for easy mashing and optimal creaminess.
- Berry variety: Use a mix of your favorite berries for a vibrant and flavorful salsa.
- Lime juice: The lime juice not only adds flavor but also helps prevent the avocado from browning.
- Seasoning: Adjust the amount of salt and pepper to your liking.

Variations:

- Spice it up: Add a pinch of red pepper flakes to the berry salsa for a hint of heat.
- Herb infusion: Incorporate fresh herbs like mint or basil into the berry salsa for a refreshing twist.
- Sweet and savory: Drizzle a tiny amount of honey or agave nectar over the berries for added sweetness (this may add points).

Why this recipe is a ZeroPoint winner:

- Nutrient-rich: Whole wheat bread provides complex carbohydrates and fiber, while avocado offers healthy fats and berries are packed with antioxidants.
- Flavorful and satisfying: The combination of creamy avocado and sweet berries creates a delicious and satisfying meal.
- Quick and easy: This recipe can be prepared in minutes, making it perfect for busy mornings or a quick snack.
- Versatile: Customize with your favorite toppings and variations to suit your taste.

Breakfast Burritos with Eggs and Salsa

These vibrant breakfast burritos are a delightful way to start your day! Packed with protein, fiber, and a burst of berry goodness, they're surprisingly creamy and satisfying, all while staying true to your ZeroPoint goals.

YIELDS: 2 SERVINGS PREP TIME: 10 MINUTES COOK TIME: 5 MINUTES

Ingredients:
- 4 large eggs
- 1/4 cup unsweetened almond milk (or any other ZeroPoint milk)
- 1/4 cup non-fat plain Greek yogurt
- 1/4 teaspoon garlic powder
- Salt and black pepper to taste
- 2 whole-wheat tortillas (look for those with the lowest points value, some may be ZeroPoint)
- 1 cup mixed berries (strawberries, raspberries, blueberries, blackberries)

- 1/4 cup chopped fresh spinach
- 1/4 cup salsa (check for ZeroPoint options, many are)

Optional toppings:
- Hot sauce (ZeroPoint)
- Chopped cilantro
- A dollop of plain Greek yogurt or avocado (in moderation)

Equipment:
- Non-stick skillet
- Spatula

Instructions:

1. Prep the Filling: In a bowl, whisk together the eggs, almond milk, Greek yogurt, garlic powder, salt, and pepper.
2. Cook the Eggs: Heat a non-stick skillet over medium heat. Pour in the egg mixture and cook, stirring occasionally, until the eggs are set and slightly creamy.
3. Warm the Tortillas: While the eggs cook, warm the tortillas in a dry skillet or microwave.
4. Assemble the Burritos: Lay the tortillas flat. Divide the scrambled eggs evenly between them. Top with the mixed berries, spinach, and salsa.
5. Roll and Enjoy: Fold the sides of the tortillas in and roll them up tightly. Serve immediately with your favorite toppings.

Tips for Success:

- Berry Blend: Use a mix of fresh or frozen berries for a variety of flavors and textures.
- Creamy Eggs: The combination of almond milk and Greek yogurt creates a luxuriously creamy texture without adding any extra points.
- Spice it Up: Add a pinch of red pepper flakes to the egg mixture for a spicy kick.
- Make it Ahead: Prepare the egg mixture and toppings the night before. In the morning, simply cook the eggs and assemble the burritos.

Why this recipe is a ZeroPoint winner:

- Protein-Packed: Eggs provide a great source of protein, keeping you full and satisfied.
- Fruit & Veggie Boost: Mixed berries and spinach contribute essential vitamins, minerals, and fiber.
- Flavorful & Versatile: Customize your burritos with different ZeroPoint toppings and salsas.
- Quick & Easy: Perfect for busy mornings when you need a healthy breakfast in a hurry.

Chapter 2

Sensational Salads

2.1 Light & Refreshing

Cucumber and Tomato Salad with Lemon Vinaigrette

This light and refreshing salad is a perfect ZeroPoint choice, packed with fresh, flavorful ingredients and a tangy vinaigrette. It's incredibly easy to prepare, making it an ideal side dish for any meal or a light lunch on its own.

YIELDS: 4 SERVINGS PREP TIME: 15 MINUTES COOK TIME: 0 MINUTES

Ingredients:
- 1 large cucumber, peeled and diced
- 4 medium tomatoes, diced
- 1/4 red onion, thinly sliced
- 1/4 cup fresh parsley, chopped
- 1/4 cup fresh dill, chopped

For the Lemon Vinaigrette:
- 2 tablespoons fresh lemon juice
- 1 tablespoon red wine vinegar
- 2 tablespoons extra virgin olive oil
- 1 teaspoon Dijon mustard
- Salt and pepper to taste

Instructions:
1. Prepare the Salad:
   - In a large bowl, combine the cucumber, tomatoes, red onion, parsley, and dill.
2. Make the Vinaigrette:
   - In a small bowl, whisk together the lemon juice, red wine vinegar, olive oil, Dijon mustard, salt, and pepper until well combined.
3. Assemble the Salad:
   - Pour the vinaigrette over the salad and toss to coat evenly.

Optional Toppings/Variations:
- Add a Crunch: Top with toasted pine nuts, sunflower seeds, or chopped almonds.
- Boost the Flavor: Add a pinch of red pepper flakes for a bit of heat.
- Fresh Herbs: Experiment with different herbs like basil, mint, or oregano.

Tips for Success:
- Use Ripe Vegetables: Ripe, juicy tomatoes and crisp cucumbers will make the salad more flavorful.
- Adjust the Vinaigrette: If you prefer a tangier dressing, add more lemon juice or vinegar. For a creamier dressing, add a teaspoon of honey.
- Serve Immediately: For the best flavor and texture, serve the salad immediately after tossing with the vinaigrette.

Why This Recipe is a ZeroPoint Winner:

This recipe is a ZeroPoint dream because it's primarily made up of non-starchy vegetables and a simple vinaigrette using zero-point ingredients like lemon juice, vinegar, and olive oil. It's a delicious and satisfying way to enjoy a guilt-free meal.

Greek Salad with Kalamata Olives and Feta

This Greek Salad is a refreshing and flavorful dish that's perfect for a light lunch or a side dish to any meal. It's packed with fresh vegetables, tangy feta cheese, and briny Kalamata olives, all of which are ZeroPoint-friendly on many plans.

YIELD: 4 SERVINGS PREP TIME: 15 MINUTES COOK TIME: 0 MINUTES

Ingredients:
- 1 large English cucumber, seeded and diced
- 4 medium tomatoes, diced
- 1 red onion, thinly sliced
- 1 green bell pepper, seeded and diced
- 1 cup Kalamata olives, pitted
- 1 cup crumbled feta cheese
- Fresh oregano, to taste
- Salt and pepper, to taste
- Extra virgin olive oil, for drizzling (optional)

Equipment:
- Large bowl
- Cutting board
- Knife

Instructions:
1. Prep the Vegetables: In a large bowl, combine the cucumber, tomatoes, red onion, and green bell pepper.

2. Add Flavor: Toss in the Kalamata olives, crumbled feta cheese, fresh oregano, salt, and pepper.
3. Serve: Serve immediately or chill for later. If desired, drizzle with a small amount of extra virgin olive oil before serving.

Optional Toppings/Variations:
- Fresh Herbs: Add fresh mint or dill for a burst of flavor.
- Lemon Juice: Squeeze fresh lemon juice over the salad for a tangy twist.
- Red Wine Vinegar: Drizzle with a high-quality red wine vinegar for a touch of acidity.
- Grilled Vegetables: Add grilled zucchini or eggplant for a smoky flavor.

Tips for Success:
- Use ripe vegetables: This will enhance the flavor of the salad.
- Cut the vegetables evenly: This will ensure that each bite is a perfect combination of flavors and textures.
- Don't overdress: A little dressing goes a long way. You can always add more if needed.

Why This Recipe is a ZeroPoint Winner:
This Greek Salad is a ZeroPoint winner because it's packed with fresh, nutrient-dense ingredients that are low in calories and high in fiber. The vegetables, feta cheese, and Kalamata olives are all ZeroPoint foods on many plans, making this a guilt-free and delicious meal option.

Strawberry Spinach Salad with Poppy Seed Dressing

This light and refreshing salad is a perfect ZeroPoint choice, packed with nutrient-rich spinach and juicy strawberries. The homemade poppy seed dressing adds a tangy sweetness that complements the fresh flavors of the salad.

YIELDS: 4 SERVINGS PREP TIME: 15 MINUTES COOK TIME: 0 MINUTES

Ingredients:
- Salad:
  - 10 cups fresh baby spinach
  - 1 pint fresh strawberries, hulled and sliced
  - 1/2 cup sliced almonds, toasted
  - 1/4 cup crumbled feta cheese
- Poppy Seed Dressing:
  - 1/4 cup red wine vinegar
  - 1/4 cup extra virgin olive oil
- 2 tablespoons honey
- 1 tablespoon poppy seeds
- 1 teaspoon Dijon mustard
- 1/2 teaspoon salt
- 1/4 teaspoon black pepper

Equipment:
- Large bowl
- Whisk
- Measuring cups and spoons

Instructions:
1. Make the Dressing: In a small bowl, whisk together the red wine vinegar, olive oil, honey, poppy seeds, Dijon mustard, salt, and pepper until well combined. Set aside.
2. Assemble the Salad: In a large bowl, combine the spinach, strawberries, and almonds.
3. Dress the Salad: Drizzle the poppy seed dressing over the salad and toss gently to coat.
4. Serve: Divide the salad among four plates and top with feta cheese. Serve immediately.

Optional Toppings/Variations:
- Add a handful of chopped pecans or walnuts for extra crunch.
- Use a different type of cheese, such as goat cheese or blue cheese.
- Add a sprinkle of dried cranberries or raspberries.
- For a sweeter dressing, increase the amount of honey.
- For a tangier dressing, increase the amount of red wine vinegar.

Tips for Success:
- Use fresh, high-quality ingredients.
- Toast the almonds to enhance their flavor and add a bit of crunch.
- Make the dressing ahead of time and store it in an airtight container in the refrigerator.
- Adjust the amount of dressing to your liking.
- Serve the salad immediately for the best flavor and texture.

Why This Recipe is a ZeroPoint Winner:
This recipe is a ZeroPoint winner because it is packed with nutrient-rich ingredients that are low in calories and high in fiber. Spinach is a great source of vitamins, minerals, and antioxidants, while strawberries are a good source of vitamin C and fiber. The poppy seed dressing is also low in calories and adds a delicious flavor to the salad.
Sources and related content

Asian Chicken Salad with Sesame Ginger Dressing

This Asian Chicken Salad is a delightful and refreshing dish that's perfect for a light lunch or a satisfying dinner. It's packed with vibrant vegetables, lean protein, and a zesty sesame ginger dressing. The best part? It's a ZeroPoint winner on many popular weight loss plans, making it a guilt-free indulgence.

YIELD: 4 SERVINGS PREP TIME: 20 MINUTES COOK TIME: 20-25 MINUTES

Ingredients:

For the Salad:

- 1 pound boneless, skinless chicken breasts
- 1 head romaine lettuce, chopped
- 1 cup shredded carrots
- 1/2 cup chopped red bell pepper
- 1/4 cup chopped green onions
- 1/4 cup sliced almonds
- 1/4 cup sesame seeds, toasted

For the Sesame Ginger Dressing:

- 1/4 cup soy sauce
- 1/4 cup rice vinegar
- 2 tablespoons fresh ginger, grated
- 2 cloves garlic, minced
- 2 tablespoons honey
- 1 tablespoon sesame oil

Equipment:

- Large bowl
- Small bowl
- Grill or skillet

Instructions:

1. Prepare the Chicken: Season the chicken breasts with salt and pepper. Grill or pan-sear until cooked through and slightly browned. Let cool, then shred.
2. Assemble the Salad: In a large bowl, combine the romaine lettuce, carrots, red bell pepper, green onions, almonds, and sesame seeds.
3. Make the Dressing: In a small bowl, whisk together the soy sauce, rice vinegar, grated ginger, minced garlic, honey, and sesame oil.
4. Combine and Serve: Add the shredded chicken to the salad. Drizzle with the sesame ginger dressing and toss to coat. Serve immediately.

Optional Toppings/Variations:

- Add chopped cilantro or mint for a fresh flavor.
- Include a handful of edamame or snap peas for extra protein.
- Top with a sprinkle of red pepper flakes for a spicy kick.
- Use a different type of lettuce, such as spinach or kale.

Tips for Success:

- For extra flavor, marinate the chicken in a mixture of soy sauce, rice vinegar, and ginger before cooking.
- Toast the sesame seeds in a dry skillet over medium heat until golden brown.
- Adjust the amount of honey in the dressing to your desired sweetness level.

Why This Recipe is a ZeroPoint Winner:

This recipe is a ZeroPoint winner because it relies on lean protein (chicken), low-calorie vegetables, and a dressing made with ingredients that are often considered ZeroPoint friendly on many popular weight loss plans. By choosing lean protein sources and non-starchy vegetables, you can create a delicious and satisfying meal that fits into your weight loss goals.

1.3 Hearty & Satisfying

Grilled Chicken Caesar Salad

This Grilled Chicken Caesar Salad is a flavorful and satisfying meal that's perfect for a quick and healthy dinner. With its perfectly grilled chicken, crisp romaine lettuce, and creamy Caesar dressing, this salad is packed with protein and nutrients. The best part? It's a ZeroPoint winner on many popular weight loss plans, making it a guilt-free indulgence.

YIELD: 4 SERVINGS PREP TIME: 15 MINUTES COOK TIME: 15 MINUTES

Ingredients:
- For the Chicken:
  - 1 pound boneless, skinless chicken breasts
  - 1 tablespoon olive oil
  - 1/2 teaspoon garlic powder
  - 1/4 teaspoon onion powder
  - 1/4 teaspoon paprika
  - Salt and pepper to taste
- For the Salad:
  - 1 head romaine lettuce, chopped
  - 1 cup croutons (store-bought or homemade)
  - 1/2 cup grated Parmesan cheese
- For the Caesar Dressing:
  - 1/4 cup mayonnaise (or Greek yogurt for a lighter option)
  - 2 tablespoons lemon juice
  - 1 clove garlic, minced
  - 1 teaspoon Dijon mustard
  - 1/4 teaspoon Worcestershire sauce
  - Salt and pepper to taste

Equipment:
- Grill or grill pan
- Large bowl

- Whisk or fork

Instructions:
1. Prepare the Chicken:
   - In a small bowl, combine olive oil, garlic powder, onion powder, paprika, salt, and pepper.
   - Rub the marinade over the chicken breasts, ensuring they are evenly coated.
   - Grill the chicken for 6-8 minutes per side, or until cooked through. Let it rest for a few minutes before slicing.
2. Make the Caesar Dressing:
   - In a small bowl, whisk together mayonnaise (or Greek yogurt), lemon juice, garlic, Dijon mustard, Worcestershire sauce, salt, and pepper until smooth.
3. Assemble the Salad:
   - In a large bowl, combine chopped romaine lettuce, croutons, and Parmesan cheese.
   - Drizzle the Caesar dressing over the salad and toss to coat.
   - Add the sliced grilled chicken to the salad and toss gently.

Optional Toppings/Variations:
- Add some crunch: Top with sliced almonds or pine nuts.
- Boost the flavor: Drizzle with a high-quality balsamic glaze.
- Make it spicy: Add a pinch of red pepper flakes to the Caesar dressing.
- Go low-carb: Substitute the croutons with additional grilled vegetables like zucchini or bell peppers.

Tips for Success:
- Don't overcook the chicken: It should be juicy and tender.
- Let the flavors meld: Allow the Caesar dressing to sit for a few minutes before using to allow the flavors to develop.
- Adjust the dressing: If the dressing is too thick, add a little more lemon juice or water to thin it out.

Why This Recipe is a ZeroPoint Winner:
This recipe is a ZeroPoint winner because it's packed with protein-rich grilled chicken and fiber-filled romaine lettuce. The Caesar dressing can be made with low-calorie ingredients like Greek yogurt, and the croutons can be homemade or purchased in a low-calorie variety. By making smart choices, you can enjoy this delicious salad without any guilt.

Salmon Nicoise Salad

This Salmon Nicoise Salad is a vibrant and flavorful dish that's perfect for any meal. It's a classic French salad, but this version is adapted to be ZeroPoint friendly, making it a guilt-free indulgence. Packed with protein, healthy fats, and fresh vegetables, this salad is both satisfying and nutritious.

YIELD: 4 SERVINGS PREP TIME: 20 MINUTES COOK TIME: 15 MINUTES

Ingredients:
- 4 skinless salmon fillets (about 4 oz each)
- 1 pound green beans, trimmed
- 4 large eggs
- 1 cup cherry tomatoes, halved
- 1/2 cup pitted kalamata olives
- 1/4 cup red onion, thinly sliced
- 2 tablespoons fresh dill, chopped
- 1 tablespoon Dijon mustard
- 2 tablespoons red wine vinegar
- 2 tablespoons olive oil
- Salt and pepper to taste
- Mixed greens (such as arugula or spring mix)

Equipment:
- Large skillet or grill pan
- Medium saucepan
- Large bowl

Instructions:
1. Cook the Salmon: Season the salmon fillets with salt and pepper. Heat a skillet over medium-high heat with a drizzle of olive oil. Cook the salmon for 4-5 minutes per side, or until it flakes easily with a fork.

2. Cook the Green Beans: Bring a pot of salted water to a boil. Add the green beans and cook for 3-4 minutes, or until crisp-tender. Drain and rinse with cold water to stop the cooking process.
3. Prepare the Eggs: Bring a pot of water to a boil. Carefully add the eggs and cook for 8-10 minutes for hard-boiled eggs. Drain and let cool before peeling.
4. Assemble the Salad: In a large bowl, combine the mixed greens, cherry tomatoes, kalamata olives, red onion, and dill.
5. Make the Dressing: In a small bowl, whisk together the Dijon mustard, red wine vinegar, and olive oil. Season with salt and pepper to taste.
6. Plate the Salad: Divide the salad mixture among four plates. Top each plate with a piece of cooked salmon, a few green beans, and a halved hard-boiled egg. Drizzle with the dressing and serve immediately.

Optional Toppings/Variations:
- Add a sprinkle of crumbled feta cheese for a creamy touch.
- Use different herbs like tarragon or chives.
- Swap out the salmon for grilled chicken or shrimp.
- Add a handful of roasted potatoes for a heartier meal.

Tips for Success:
- For perfectly cooked salmon, use a meat thermometer. It should reach an internal temperature of 145°F (63°C).
- Don't overcook the green beans. They should be crisp-tender.
- Make the dressing ahead of time and store it in the refrigerator.
- Assemble the salad just before serving to keep the greens crisp.

Why This Recipe is a ZeroPoint Winner:
This Salmon Nicoise Salad is a ZeroPoint winner because it's packed with protein-rich salmon, fiber-filled vegetables, and healthy fats from the olive oil and avocado. It's a delicious and satisfying meal that won't derail your weight loss goals.

Black Bean and Corn Salad with Avocado Dressing

This vibrant and flavorful salad is a ZeroPoint dream come true! Packed with protein-rich black beans, fiber-filled corn, and healthy fats from avocados, this dish is both satisfying and guilt-free. Perfect for a quick lunch or a side dish for dinner, this recipe is easy to customize and always a crowd-pleaser.

YIELDS: 4 SERVINGS PREP TIME: 15 MINUTES COOK TIME: 0 MINUTES

Ingredients:

- 1 can (15 ounces) black beans, rinsed and drained
- 1 cup fresh or frozen corn kernels
- 1/2 red onion, finely chopped
- 1/2 bell pepper, diced
- 1/4 cup fresh cilantro, chopped
- 1 lime, juiced

For the Avocado Dressing:

- 1 ripe avocado
- 1/4 cup fresh lime juice
-

- 1 tablespoon extra virgin olive oil
- 1/2 teaspoon chili powder
- 1/4 teaspoon cumin
- Salt and pepper to taste

Equipment:

- Large bowl
- Small bowl
- Fork
- Knife
- Cutting board

Instructions:
1. Prepare the Salad:
    - In a large bowl, combine black beans, corn, red onion, bell pepper, and cilantro.
    - Stir to combine.
2. Make the Avocado Dressing:
    - In a small bowl, mash the avocado with a fork until smooth.
    - Add lime juice, olive oil, chili powder, cumin, salt, and pepper.
    - Stir until well combined.
3. Assemble the Salad:
    - Pour the avocado dressing over the salad and toss to coat.

Optional Toppings/Variations:
- Add diced tomatoes or jalapeños for extra flavor.
- Sprinkle with crumbled feta cheese or cotija cheese.
- Serve over lettuce leaves for a low-carb option.

Tips for Success:
- Use ripe avocados for the creamiest dressing.
- Adjust the spice level to your preference by adding more or less chili powder and cumin.
- For a quicker prep, use a pre-cooked rotisserie chicken.

Why This Recipe is a ZeroPoint Winner:
This recipe is packed with ZeroPoint foods like black beans, corn, and cilantro. The avocado dressing adds healthy fats and flavor without breaking the bank on Points. By focusing on whole, unprocessed foods, you can enjoy a delicious and satisfying meal without sacrificing your weight loss goals.

Quinoa and Roasted Vegetable Salad

This vibrant and flavorful salad is a ZeroPoint dream! Packed with colorful, nutrient-dense vegetables and protein-rich quinoa, it's a satisfying and guilt-free meal.

YIELD: 4 SERVINGS PREP TIME: 20 MINUTES COOK TIME: 30-40 MINUTES

Ingredients:
- 1 cup quinoa, rinsed
- 2 cups mixed vegetables (such as broccoli florets, bell pepper chunks, and cherry tomatoes)
- 1 tablespoon olive oil
- 1/2 teaspoon salt
- 1/4 teaspoon black pepper
- Fresh herbs (such as basil, cilantro, or mint), chopped

Equipment:
- Large bowl
- Baking sheet
- Pot with lid

Instructions:
1. Prep the Vegetables: Preheat your oven to 400°F (200°C). Toss the mixed vegetables with olive oil, salt, and pepper on a baking sheet. Spread them out in a single layer.
2. Roast the Vegetables: Roast the vegetables in the preheated oven for 25-30 minutes, or until tender-crisp and slightly browned.
3. Cook the Quinoa: While the vegetables are roasting, cook the quinoa according to package directions. Fluff with a fork and set aside to cool.

4. Assemble the Salad: Once the quinoa and vegetables have cooled, combine them in a large bowl. Add fresh herbs and toss gently to combine.

Optional Toppings/Variations:
- Add a squeeze of lemon juice for a bright, tangy flavor.
- Sprinkle with crumbled feta cheese or toasted nuts for extra crunch and flavor.
- Drizzle with a light vinaigrette for a touch of acidity.
- Use different vegetables, such as zucchini, eggplant, or sweet potatoes.

Tips for Success:
- Don't overcrowd the baking sheet when roasting vegetables. This will ensure even cooking.
- For extra flavor, roast the vegetables with a sprinkle of your favorite spices, such as cumin, paprika, or garlic powder.
- If you prefer a warm salad, serve it immediately after assembling. For a cold salad, let it chill in the refrigerator for a few hours.

Why This Recipe is a ZeroPoint Winner:
This recipe is packed with ZeroPoint foods like vegetables and quinoa, making it a guilt-free and satisfying meal. It's easy to customize with your favorite ingredients, so you can enjoy it in countless ways.

Chapter 3

Souperbly Delicious Soups

Creamy & Comforting

Roasted Tomato Soup with Grilled Cheese Croutons

This hearty and flavorful soup is a perfect ZeroPoint winner because it relies on fresh, flavorful ingredients and simple cooking techniques. The roasted tomatoes add a rich, smoky depth, while the grilled cheese croutons provide a satisfying crunch.

YIELD: 4 SERVINGS PREP TIME: 20 MINUTES COOK TIME: 45 MINUTES

Ingredients:

For the Soup:

- 2 pounds ripe tomatoes, halved
- 1 large onion, quartered
- 4 cloves garlic, peeled
- 1 tablespoon olive oil
- 4 cups vegetable broth
- 1 teaspoon dried basil
- 1/2 teaspoon dried oregano
- Salt and pepper to taste

For the Grilled Cheese Croutons:

- 4 slices whole-grain bread
- 1 tablespoon unsalted butter, softened
- 1/4 cup shredded cheese (like cheddar or mozzarella)

Equipment:

- Large baking sheet
- Rimmed baking sheet
- Large pot
- Immersion blender or regular blender
- Skillet

Instructions:

1. Roast the Vegetables: Preheat oven to 425°F (220°C). Toss tomatoes, onion, and garlic with olive oil, salt, and pepper on a large baking sheet. Roast for 30-35 minutes, or until vegetables are softened and slightly charred.

2. Make the Soup: While the vegetables are roasting, bring the vegetable broth to a simmer in a large pot.

3. Blend the Soup: Transfer the roasted vegetables to a blender or use an immersion blender to puree until smooth. Add the pureed vegetables to the simmering broth, along with the dried basil and oregano. Season with salt and pepper to taste.

4. Make the Grilled Cheese Croutons: Spread butter on one side of each slice of bread. Place the buttered side down on a rimmed baking sheet. Top each slice with shredded cheese. Broil for 2-3 minutes, or until the cheese is melted and bubbly. Cut each slice into 4 croutons.

5. Serve: Ladle the soup into bowls and top with grilled cheese croutons.

Optional Toppings/Variations:

- Fresh basil
- A drizzle of balsamic vinegar
- A sprinkle of red pepper flakes
- A dollop of Greek yogurt

Tips for Success:

- For a richer flavor, consider roasting a red bell pepper along with the tomatoes and onions.
- If you don't have an immersion blender, transfer the soup to a regular blender in batches and blend until smooth. Be careful when blending hot liquids.
- For a vegan version, use a non-dairy butter and cheese alternative.

Why This Recipe is a ZeroPoint Winner:

This recipe is packed with flavor and nutrients, all while keeping your ZeroPoint count low. The vegetables are the stars of the show, providing essential vitamins, minerals, and fiber. The grilled cheese croutons add a satisfying crunch and a touch of indulgence without breaking the ZeroPoint bank.

Creamy Cauliflower Soup with Chives

This creamy cauliflower soup is a ZeroPoint dream! It's packed with flavor, incredibly satisfying, and guilt-free. The secret to its velvety texture lies in blending the cauliflower until smooth, creating a rich and creamy soup without any added cream or dairy.

YIELD: 4 SERVINGS PREP TIME: 15 MINUTES COOK TIME: 30 MINUTES

Ingredients:
- 1 large head of cauliflower, cut into florets
- 1 onion, chopped
- 2 cloves garlic, minced
- 4 cups vegetable broth
- 1 teaspoon salt
- 1/2 teaspoon black pepper
- Fresh chives, for garnish

Equipment:
- Large pot
- Immersion blender or regular blender

Instructions:
1. Sauté the Aromatics: Heat a large pot over medium heat. Add the onion and garlic, and sauté until softened and fragrant, about 5 minutes.
2. Add the Cauliflower and Broth: Add the cauliflower florets, vegetable broth, salt, and pepper to the pot. Bring to a boil, then reduce heat and simmer, covered, for 20-25 minutes, or until the cauliflower is very tender.
3. Blend the Soup: Carefully transfer the soup to a blender or use an immersion blender to puree until smooth and creamy. If using a regular blender, blend in batches.
4. Serve: Pour the soup into bowls and garnish with fresh chives.

Optional Toppings/Variations:

- Crispy Bacon: Add a few pieces of crispy bacon for a smoky, savory flavor.
- Roasted Garlic: Roast a few cloves of garlic and add them to the soup for a deeper flavor.
- Herbs: Experiment with different herbs like thyme, rosemary, or sage.
- Spicy Kick: Add a pinch of red pepper flakes for a bit of heat.

Tips for Success:

- Don't Overcook the Cauliflower: Overcooked cauliflower can become watery.
- Blend Until Smooth: The smoother the blend, the creamier the soup.
- Adjust Seasonings: Taste the soup and adjust the salt and pepper as needed.

Why This Recipe is a ZeroPoint Winner:

Cauliflower is a versatile vegetable that's incredibly low in points. This recipe utilizes its natural creaminess to create a delicious and satisfying soup without the need for any high-point ingredients. It's a perfect choice for anyone following a ZeroPoint plan who wants to enjoy a hearty and flavorful meal

Butternut Squash Soup with Ginger and Apple

This creamy, comforting soup is a perfect ZeroPoint choice, packed with flavor and nutrients. The combination of sweet butternut squash, tart apple, and spicy ginger creates a harmonious blend that's both satisfying and guilt-free.

Yields: 4 servings Prep time: 20 minutes Cook time: 30-35 minutes

Ingredients:

- 1 large butternut squash, peeled, seeded, and cubed
- 1 large apple, peeled, cored, and chopped
- 1 onion, chopped
- 2 cloves garlic, minced
- 1 inch piece of ginger, grated
- 4 cups vegetable broth
- Salt and pepper to taste
- Optional toppings: Greek yogurt, chopped fresh herbs, toasted pumpkin seeds

Equipment:

- Large pot
- Immersion blender or regular blender

Instructions:

1. Sauté the Aromatics: Heat a large pot over medium heat. Add the onion and garlic, and cook until softened, about 5 minutes. Stir in the grated ginger and cook for an additional 30 seconds.
2. Add the Vegetables and Broth: Add the cubed butternut squash, chopped apple, and vegetable broth to the pot. Bring to a boil, then reduce heat and simmer, covered, for 25-30 minutes, or until the vegetables are tender.

3. Blend the Soup: Use an immersion blender to puree the soup directly in the pot, or transfer the soup to a regular blender and blend until smooth.
4. Season and Serve: Season the soup with salt and pepper to taste. Serve hot, topped with Greek yogurt, fresh herbs, or toasted pumpkin seeds, if desired.

Optional Variations:
- Spicy Kick: Add a pinch of cayenne pepper or red pepper flakes to the soup for a bit of heat.
- Creamy Texture: For a creamier soup, stir in a dollop of Greek yogurt or a splash of coconut milk.
- Hearty Meal: Serve the soup with a side of whole-grain bread or a grilled cheese sandwich.

Tips for Success:
- Roasting the Squash: For a deeper flavor, roast the butternut squash before adding it to the soup.
- Adjust the Spice Level: If you prefer a milder flavor, reduce the amount of ginger used.
- Store Leftovers: Store leftover soup in an airtight container in the refrigerator for up to 3 days.

Why This Recipe is a ZeroPoint Winner:
This Butternut Squash Soup is a ZeroPoint dream because it's packed with flavor and nutrients, yet it's low in calories and fat. The vegetables are naturally low in Points, and the broth and spices add minimal Points. By choosing zero-point toppings like herbs and spices, you can enjoy a delicious and satisfying meal without breaking your Points budget.

Curried Lentil Soup with Coconut Milk

This hearty and flavorful Curried Lentil Soup is a ZeroPoint dream come true! Packed with protein-rich lentils and creamy coconut milk, it's a satisfying and nutritious meal that won't cost you a single point. The fragrant blend of curry spices adds a warm and comforting touch to this delicious soup.

YIELD: 6 SERVINGS PREP TIME: 10 MINUTES COOK TIME: 30-35 MINUTES

Ingredients:

- 1 tablespoon olive oil
- 1 onion, chopped
- 2 cloves garlic, minced
- 1 teaspoon ground cumin
- 1 teaspoon curry powder
- 1/2 teaspoon red pepper flakes (adjust to taste)
- 4 cups vegetable broth
- 1 can (13.5 oz) unsweetened coconut milk
- 1 cup red lentils, rinsed
- Salt and pepper to taste
- Fresh cilantro, for garnish

Equipment:

- Large pot
- Cutting board
- Knife

Instructions:

1. Sauté the Aromatics: Heat the olive oil in a large pot over medium heat. Add the onion and garlic, and cook until softened, about 5 minutes.

2. Add Spices and Liquid: Stir in the cumin, curry powder, and red pepper flakes. Cook for 30 seconds more, or until fragrant. Pour in the vegetable broth and coconut milk.
3. Simmer the Soup: Bring the mixture to a boil, then reduce heat and simmer, uncovered, for 25-30 minutes, or until the lentils are tender.
4. Season and Serve: Season with salt and pepper to taste. Garnish with fresh cilantro and serve hot.

Optional Toppings/Variations:
- Spicy Kick: Add a pinch of cayenne pepper or a drizzle of hot sauce.
- Creamy Texture: Blend a portion of the soup for a smoother consistency.
- Hearty Meal: Serve with a side of crusty bread or a dollop of Greek yogurt.

Tips for Success:
- Rinse the Lentils: Rinsing the lentils before cooking helps remove any impurities and prevents the soup from becoming cloudy.
- Adjust the Spice Level: If you prefer a milder flavor, reduce the amount of red pepper flakes or omit it altogether.
- Store Leftovers: Store any leftovers in an airtight container in the refrigerator for up to 3 days.

Why This Recipe is a ZeroPoint Winner:
This recipe primarily features ZeroPoint foods like lentils, vegetables, and spices. The coconut milk, while not ZeroPoint, is used in moderation and contributes to the rich flavor and creamy texture of the soup. By focusing on these ZeroPoint ingredients and mindful portion control, you can enjoy this delicious and satisfying meal without worrying about breaking the bank on your Points budget.

Sources and related content

Chapter 4

Entrées That Excite

Poultry Perfection

Lemon Herb Roasted Chicken

This Lemon Herb Roasted Chicken is a delicious and healthy dish that is perfect for any occasion. It is made with simple ingredients that are easy to find, and it is cooked in a way that is both healthy and flavorful. The chicken is roasted in the oven with lemon, herbs, and garlic, which gives it a delicious flavor. This recipe is also a ZeroPoint winner, which means that it is low in calories and fat.

YIELD: 4-6 SERVINGS PREP TIME: 20 MINUTES COOK TIME: 1 HOUR 20 MINUTES

Ingredients:

- 1 (3-4 pound) whole chicken
- 1 lemon, cut into wedges
- 1 head of garlic, cloves separated and peeled
- 1 tablespoon olive oil
- 1 teaspoon dried thyme
- 1/2 teaspoon dried rosemary
- 1/4 teaspoon salt
- 1/4 teaspoon black pepper

Equipment:

- Roasting pan
- Basting spoon

Instructions:

1. Preheat oven to 425 degrees F (220 degrees C).
2. Rinse chicken inside and out with cold water. Pat dry with paper towels.
3. Place chicken in roasting pan, breast side up.
4. Stuff cavity of chicken with lemon wedges and garlic cloves.
5. Drizzle chicken with olive oil.
6. Sprinkle chicken with thyme, rosemary, salt, and pepper.
7. Roast chicken in preheated oven for 1 hour 20 minutes, or until juices run clear when thigh is pierced with a fork.
8. Remove chicken from oven and let rest for 10 minutes before carving.

Optional Toppings/Variations:

- Serve with roasted vegetables, such as potatoes, carrots, or Brussels sprouts.
- Add other herbs to the recipe, such as sage, oregano, or basil.
- Use different citrus fruits, such as oranges or grapefruits.

Tips for Success:

- Let the chicken come to room temperature before roasting.
- Don't overcrowd the roasting pan.
- Baste the chicken every 20 minutes with the pan juices.
- Let the chicken rest for 10 minutes before carving.

Why This Recipe is a ZeroPoint Winner:

This recipe is a ZeroPoint winner because it is low in calories and fat. The chicken is roasted in the oven, which helps to keep it lean. The lemon, herbs, and garlic add flavor without adding calories or fat. This recipe is a great way to enjoy a delicious and healthy meal.

Grilled Chicken with Mango Salsa

Grilled chicken is a classic dish that is both delicious and healthy. It is a great source of protein and can be enjoyed by people of all ages. Mango salsa is a refreshing and flavorful side dish that is the perfect complement to grilled chicken. This recipe is a ZeroPoint winner because it is low in calories and carbohydrates, and it is packed with protein and fiber.

YIELD: 4 SERVINGS PREP TIME: 15 MINUTES COOK TIME: 20-25 MINUTES

Ingredients:

- 1 pound boneless, skinless chicken breasts
- 1/2 teaspoon salt
- 1/4 teaspoon black pepper
- 1/4 teaspoon garlic powder
- 1/4 teaspoon onion powder
- 1/4 teaspoon paprika
- 1/4 teaspoon cayenne pepper
- 1 ripe mango, peeled, pitted, and diced
- 1/2 red onion, diced
- 1/2 cup chopped fresh cilantro
- 1/4 cup lime juice
- 1/4 teaspoon salt
- 1/8 teaspoon black pepper

Equipment:

- Grill
- Skewers (optional)
- Cutting board
- Knife
- Mixing bowl

Instructions:

1. Preheat the grill to medium-high heat.
2. In a small bowl, combine the salt, pepper, garlic powder, onion powder, paprika, and cayenne pepper.
3. Season the chicken breasts with the spice mixture.
4. If using skewers, thread the chicken onto the skewers.
5. Grill the chicken for 10-12 minutes per side, or until cooked through.
6. While the chicken is grilling, prepare the mango salsa.
7. In a medium bowl, combine the mango, red onion, cilantro, lime juice, salt, and pepper.
8. Toss to combine.
9. Serve the grilled chicken with the mango salsa.

Optional Toppings/Variations:

- Add your favorite vegetables to the skewers, such as bell peppers, mushrooms, or zucchini.
- Use different types of salsa, such as pineapple salsa or tomato salsa.
- Top the chicken with avocado or crumbled feta cheese.

Tips for Success:

- Don't overcrowd the grill. Cook the chicken in batches if necessary.
- Use a meat thermometer to ensure that the chicken is cooked through. The internal temperature should reach 165°F (74°C).
- Let the chicken rest for a few minutes before slicing. This will help the juices redistribute.

Why This Recipe is a ZeroPoint Winner:

This recipe is a ZeroPoint winner because it is low in calories and carbohydrates, and it is packed with protein and fiber. Chicken is a great source of protein, and mango is a good source of fiber and vitamin C. This recipe is also easy to make and can be customized to your liking.

Chicken Stir-Fry with Brown Rice

This delicious and healthy chicken stir-fry is a great way to enjoy a flavorful and satisfying meal without any ZeroPoints. The chicken is cooked to perfection, the vegetables are crisp-tender, and the brown rice is fluffy and delicious. This recipe is easy to make and can be customized to your liking.

YIELD: 4 SERVINGS PREP TIME: 15 MINUTES COOK TIME: 20 MINUTES

Ingredients:

- 1 pound boneless, skinless chicken breast, cut into bite-sized pieces
- 1 tablespoon cornstarch
- 1 teaspoon soy sauce
- 1/2 teaspoon sesame oil
- 1/4 teaspoon garlic powder
- 1/4 teaspoon ginger powder
- 1 cup broccoli florets
- 1 cup carrots, sliced
- 1/2 cup snow peas
- 1/2 cup onion, sliced
- 1/4 cup water
- 1/4 cup low-sodium chicken broth
- 1 tablespoon cornstarch
- 1 teaspoon soy sauce
- 1/2 teaspoon sesame oil
- 1/4 teaspoon garlic powder
- 1/4 teaspoon ginger powder
- 1 cup cooked brown rice

Equipment:

- Large skillet or wok
- Measuring cups and spoons
- Cutting board
- Knife

Instructions:

1. In a medium bowl, combine the chicken, cornstarch, soy sauce, sesame oil, garlic powder, and ginger powder. Stir to coat the chicken evenly.
2. Heat a large skillet or wok over medium-high heat. Add the chicken and cook for 5-7 minutes, or until the chicken is cooked through.
3. Add the broccoli, carrots, snow peas, and onion to the skillet. Cook for 5 minutes, or until the vegetables are crisp-tender.
4. In a small bowl, whisk together the water, chicken broth, cornstarch, soy sauce, sesame oil, garlic powder, and ginger powder.
5. Pour the sauce over the chicken and vegetables. Bring to a boil, then reduce heat to low and simmer for 2 minutes, or until the sauce has thickened.
6. Serve the chicken stir-fry over cooked brown rice.

Optional toppings/variations:

*   Add your favorite vegetables to the stir-fry.
*   Use a different type of protein, such as shrimp or tofu.
*   Serve the stir-fry over noodles or quinoa.

Tips for success:

*   Cut the chicken into bite-sized pieces so that it cooks evenly.
*   Don't overcrowd the skillet when cooking the chicken and vegetables.
*   Make sure to whisk the sauce ingredients together until smooth before adding them to the skillet.
*   Serve the stir-fry immediately so that the sauce doesn't thicken too much.

Why this recipe is a ZeroPoint winner:

This recipe is a ZeroPoint winner because it is made with lean protein, low-calorie vegetables, and whole grains. It is also easy to make and can be customized to your liking.

Chicken Fajitas with Bell Peppers and Onions

This recipe for ZeroPoint Chicken Fajitas with Bell Peppers and Onions is a delicious and healthy way to enjoy your favorite Mexican dish. Fajitas are traditionally made with steak or chicken, but this recipe uses chicken breast, which is a lean protein that is low in calories and fat. The bell peppers and onions add flavor and nutrients, and the tortillas are a great source of carbohydrates.

YIELD: 4 SERVINGS PREP TIME: 15 MINUTES COOK TIME: 20 MINUTES

Ingredients:

- 1 pound boneless, skinless chicken breast, cut into 1-inch cubes
- 1 red bell pepper, seeded and cut into 1-inch pieces
- 1 green bell pepper, seeded and cut into 1-inch pieces
- 1 onion, cut into 1-inch pieces
- 1 teaspoon chili powder
- 1/2 teaspoon cumin
- 1/4 teaspoon garlic powder
- 1/4 teaspoon salt
- 1/8 teaspoon black pepper
- 1 lime, juiced

Equipment:

- Large skillet
- Tongs
- Cutting board
- Knife

Instructions:

1. Season the chicken with chili powder, cumin, garlic powder, salt, and pepper.

2. Heat a large skillet over medium heat. Add the chicken and cook until browned on all sides.
3. Add the bell peppers and onions to the skillet and cook until softened.
4. Add the lime juice to the skillet and stir to combine.
5. Serve the chicken fajitas with your favorite toppings, such as salsa, guacamole, sour cream, and cheese.

Optional Toppings/Variations:
- Salsa
- Guacamole
- Sour cream
- Cheese
- Cilantro
- Limes

Tips for Success:
- To make the chicken extra tender, marinate it in lime juice and spices for at least 30 minutes before cooking.
- For a spicier fajita, add a pinch of cayenne pepper to the chicken seasoning.
- If you don't have lime juice, you can use lemon juice or white vinegar.
- Serve the fajitas with your favorite tortillas, such as flour tortillas, corn tortillas, or whole wheat tortillas.

Why This Recipe is a ZeroPoint Winner:
This recipe is a ZeroPoint winner because it is low in calories and fat, and it is packed with protein, vitamins, and minerals. The chicken is a lean protein source, and the bell peppers and onions are good sources of fiber and vitamins A and C. The lime juice adds a refreshing flavor and helps to boost the immune system.

Additional Tips:
- To make this recipe even healthier, use whole wheat tortillas or corn tortillas.
- If you are watching your sodium intake, you can use less salt when seasoning the chicken.
- This recipe can be easily customized to your liking. You can add or subtract any of the ingredients to create your own unique fajita.

Chapter 5

Side Dish Stars

Vegetable Variety

Roasted Brussels Sprouts with Balsamic Glaze

Brussels sprouts are a versatile and nutritious vegetable that can be enjoyed in many different ways. One of the most popular ways to prepare them is to roast them in the oven until they are crispy and golden brown. This recipe for Roasted Brussels Sprouts with Balsamic Glaze is a delicious and healthy way to enjoy this wintertime favorite.

YIELD: 4 SERVINGS PREP TIME: 10 MINUTES COOK TIME: 25-30 MINUTES

Ingredients:	1/4 cup balsamic vinegar
• 1 pound Brussels sprouts, trimmed and halved • 2 tablespoons olive oil • 1/2 teaspoon salt • 1/4 teaspoon black pepper •	**Equipment:** • Large bowl • Rimmed baking sheet • Parchment paper • Small saucepan

Instructions:

1. Preheat oven to 400 degrees F (200 degrees C).
2. In a large bowl, toss Brussels sprouts with olive oil, salt, and pepper until evenly coated.
3. Spread Brussels sprouts in a single layer on a rimmed baking sheet lined with parchment paper.
4. Roast for 25-30 minutes, or until Brussels sprouts are golden brown and tender.
5. While Brussels sprouts are roasting, heat balsamic vinegar in a small saucepan over medium heat. Bring to a boil, then reduce heat to low and simmer until vinegar has thickened slightly, about 5 minutes.
6. Remove Brussels sprouts from oven and drizzle with balsamic glaze. Serve immediately.

Optional toppings/variations:

- Toasted pine nuts
- Shredded Parmesan cheese
- Bacon bits
- Red pepper flakes
- Fresh herbs, such as thyme or rosemary

Tips for success:

- Don't overcrowd the baking sheet. Brussels sprouts should be in a single layer so that they roast evenly.
- Don't overcook the Brussels sprouts. They should be tender but still have a slight crunch.
- If the balsamic glaze is too thick, you can thin it out with a little water or vinegar.

Why this recipe is a ZeroPoint winner:

This recipe is a ZeroPoint winner because it is low in calories and carbohydrates, and high in fiber and other nutrients. Brussels sprouts are a good source of vitamins C and K, as well as folate and potassium. They are also a good source of fiber, which can help to promote digestive health. Balsamic vinegar is a good source of antioxidants, which can help to protect the body from damage caused by free radicals.

Garlic Roasted Asparagus

This simple yet flavorful recipe is a ZeroPoint dream! Roasting brings out the natural sweetness of asparagus, while the garlic adds a delicious savory punch.

YIELDS: 4 SERVINGS PREP TIME: 10 MINUTES COOK TIME: 15-20 MINUTES

Ingredients:

- 1 pound asparagus, trimmed
- 2 cloves garlic, minced
- 1 tablespoon olive oil
- Salt and pepper to taste

Equipment:

- Baking sheet
- Parchment paper

Instructions:

1. Preheat Oven: Preheat your oven to 425°F (220°C).
2. Prepare Asparagus: Trim the woody ends of the asparagus spears.
3. Season Asparagus: In a large bowl, toss the asparagus with minced garlic, olive oil, salt, and pepper.
4. Roast Asparagus: Spread the seasoned asparagus on a parchment-lined baking sheet.
5. Bake: Roast in the preheated oven for 15-20 minutes, or until tender-crisp.

6. Serve: Serve immediately.

Optional Toppings/Variations:
- Lemon Zest: A sprinkle of lemon zest adds a bright, citrusy flavor.
- Red Pepper Flakes: For a bit of heat, add a pinch of red pepper flakes.
- Parmesan Cheese: A light dusting of Parmesan cheese adds a savory, umami flavor.

Tips for Success:
- Don't Overcook: Overcooking can lead to mushy asparagus.
- Choose Fresh Asparagus: Fresh asparagus will have a brighter green color and will be crisp.
- Don't overcrowd the pan: If you're roasting a large batch, consider using two baking sheets to prevent overcrowding.

Why This Recipe is a ZeroPoint Winner:
This recipe is a ZeroPoint winner because it's made with simple, whole ingredients that are low in calories and high in nutrients. Asparagus is a great source of fiber, vitamins, and minerals, and it's a versatile vegetable that can be enjoyed in many different ways.
Sources and related content

Sautéed Spinach with Garlic

This simple yet flavorful dish is a ZeroPoint winner because it's primarily made up of spinach, a leafy green vegetable that's incredibly low in calories and packed with essential nutrients. The addition of garlic, a flavor powerhouse, adds depth without significantly impacting the calorie count.

YIELDS: 4 SERVINGS PREP TIME: 5 MINUTES COOK TIME: 5 MINUTES

Ingredients:
• 1 pound fresh spinach, washed and stemmed
• 2 cloves garlic, minced
• 1 tablespoon olive oil
• Salt and pepper to taste

Equipment:
• Large skillet or sauté pan

Instructions:

1. Heat the oil: Heat the olive oil in a large skillet over medium heat.
2. Sauté the garlic: Add the minced garlic to the hot oil and sauté for about 30 seconds, or until fragrant.

3. Add the spinach: Add the washed spinach to the skillet, stirring to coat with the garlic oil.
4. Cook the spinach: Cover the skillet and cook for 2-3 minutes, or until the spinach is wilted.
5. Season: Season with salt and pepper to taste.
6. Serve: Serve immediately.

Optional Toppings/Variations:
- Lemon Zest: Add a bright, citrusy flavor by grating lemon zest over the finished dish.
- Red Pepper Flakes: For a bit of heat, sprinkle red pepper flakes over the spinach.
- Pine Nuts: Add a nutty crunch by sprinkling toasted pine nuts on top.

Tips for Success:
- Don't Overcook: Overcooking spinach can make it mushy. Cook it just until it's wilted.
- Fresh is Best: Use fresh spinach for the best flavor and texture.
- Don't overcrowd the pan: If you have a large amount of spinach, cook it in batches to prevent overcrowding the pan.

Why This Recipe is a ZeroPoint Winner: This recipe is a ZeroPoint dream because spinach is considered a free food on many weight loss plans. It's low in calories, high in nutrients, and incredibly versatile. By keeping the ingredients simple and the cooking method straightforward, you can enjoy a delicious and healthy meal without any guilt.

Sweet Potato Fries with Chipotle Mayo

Sweet potato fries are a delicious and healthy alternative to regular french fries. They are lower in calories and fat than regular fries and are a good source of fiber and vitamins. Chipotle mayo is a flavorful and spicy dipping sauce that is perfect for sweet potato fries. This recipe is a ZeroPoint winner because it is made with simple, healthy ingredients and is low in calories and fat.

YIELD: 4 SERVINGS PREP TIME: 15 MINUTES COOK TIME: 25 MINUTES

Ingredients:
- Sweet potatoes: 2 large sweet potatoes, peeled and cut into thin strips
- Olive oil: 1 tablespoon
- Salt and pepper: to taste
- Chipotle peppers in adobo sauce: 2 tablespoons
- Mayonnaise: 1/4 cup
- Lime juice: 1 tablespoon
- Cilantro: 1/4 cup, chopped

Equipment:
- Large bowl
- Baking sheet
- Parchment paper
- Small bowl
- Whisk

Instructions:
1. Preheat oven to 425 degrees F (220 degrees C).
2. In a large bowl, toss sweet potatoes with olive oil, salt, and pepper.

3. Spread sweet potatoes in a single layer on a baking sheet lined with parchment paper.
4. Bake for 20-25 minutes, or until golden brown and crispy.
5. While sweet potatoes are baking, make the chipotle mayo.
6. In a small bowl, whisk together chipotle peppers, mayonnaise, lime juice, and cilantro.
7. Serve sweet potato fries with chipotle mayo.

Optional toppings/variations:
- Add your favorite spices to the sweet potatoes, such as garlic powder, onion powder, or paprika.
- Use a different type of oil, such as avocado oil or coconut oil.
- Add other ingredients to the chipotle mayo, such as lime zest, jalapeños, or honey.
- Serve sweet potato fries with other dipping sauces, such as ketchup, mustard, or ranch dressing.

Tips for success:
- Cut sweet potatoes into thin strips for even cooking.
- Don't overcrowd the baking sheet.
- Flip sweet potatoes halfway through cooking.
- Serve sweet potato fries immediately.

Why this recipe is a ZeroPoint winner:
This recipe is a ZeroPoint winner because it is made with simple, healthy ingredients and is low in calories and fat. Sweet potatoes are a good source of fiber and vitamins, and chipotle mayo is a flavorful and spicy dipping sauce that is made with healthy ingredients.

BONUS SECTION

Meal Plan: A 4-Week Culinary Adventure

Week 1	Week 2	Week 3	Week 4
Monday	Monday	Monday	Monday
Berry Blast Smoothie Bowl	Greek Salad with Kalamata Olives and Feta	Roasted Tomato Soup with Grilled Cheese Croutons	Spinach and Feta Omelet
Tuesday	Tuesday	Tuesday	Tuesday
Savory Oatmeal Power Bowl with Eggs	Grilled Chicken Caesar Salad	Creamy Cauliflower Soup with Chives	Smoked Salmon and Avocado Scramble
Wednesday	Wednesday	Wednesday	Wednesday
Southwest Quinoa Power Bowl	Strawberry Spinach Salad with Poppy Seed Dressing	Butternut Squash Soup with Ginger and Apple	Veggie-Packed Frittata
Thursday	Thursday	Thursday	Thursday
Egg-cellent Creations: Spinach and Feta Omelet	Asian Chicken Salad with Sesame Ginger Dressing	Curried Lentil Soup with Coconut Milk	Mushroom and Gruyere Quiche
Friday	Friday	Friday	Friday
Smoked Salmon and Avocado Scramble	Black Bean and Corn Salad with Avocado Dressing	Berry Blast Smoothie Bowl	Overnight Oats with Berries and Nuts
Saturday	Saturday	Saturday	Saturday
Veggie-Packed Frittata	Quinoa and Roasted Vegetable Salad	Greek Salad with Kalamata Olives and Feta	Yogurt Parfaits with Granola and Fruit
Sunday	Sunday	Sunday	Sunday
Mushroom and Gruyere Quiche	Roasted Tomato Soup with Grilled Cheese Croutons	Creamy Cauliflower Soup with Chives	Whole Wheat Toast with Avocado and Tomato

Metric Conversion Chart

US Measurement Metric Equivalent

1 cup (liquid)	237 ml
1 cup (dry)	240 ml
1 tablespoon	15 ml
1 teaspoon	5 ml
1 pound	454 g
1 ounce	28.35 g
1 quart	946 ml
1 gallon	3.785 liters
1 inch	2.54 cm

Tips for Converting:
1. Use a Kitchen Scale: A kitchen scale is the most accurate tool for measuring ingredients in grams.
2. Online Conversion Tools: Many online tools can help you convert measurements quickly and accurately.
3. Adjustments: When converting, you may need to adjust cooking times and temperatures slightly.
4. Volume vs. Weight: Be aware that volume measurements can vary depending on the density of the ingredient. For more precise measurements, use weight.

Additional Considerations:
- Temperature: Fahrenheit to Celsius conversion: $°C = (°F - 32) / 1.8$
- Oven Temperature: Adjust oven temperatures slightly, as metric ovens may have slightly different heat distribution.
- Baking: Baking recipes can be more sensitive to measurement changes. Consider using a reliable conversion tool or recipe specifically designed for metric measurements.